gooseflesh

poetry by

Emma Morgan

with illustrations by Sudie Rakusin

Clothespin Fever Press
San Diego   1993

Cataloging information:
Morgan, Emma
          Gooseflesh
1. Title

811.54   1993   ISBN: 1-878533-06-1

"The Words I Want" and "Chill" first appeared in *Bay Windows*, Vol. 9

"Shluf Gezunt" was previously published by Sidewalk Revolution Press in the anthology *Wanting Women*.

Cover artist: Sudie Rakusin
Photo of author on back cover: Tam Garson

Acknowledgements

Special thanks to my friend (and number one fan) Amelia Haviland, who cajoled me into my first public reading, attended my next eight readings thereafter and booked me my first paid gig. A great, big thank you to the Valley Lesbian Writers Group— you have been my "school without walls" since I was twenty-two, and I hope I never graduate. Thank you to Jenny Wrenn and Carolyn Weathers for the literary midwifery that brought this book into being, Sudie Rakusin for her artwork and Tam Garson for the photo of me on the back cover. Thank you to Linda Mullis for making sure I didn't fall through a hole in the flag along the way and to my cat, Aeton, who loves me and lets me pet him when I'm thinking.

This book is dedicated to all of the women who . . .
well, to all of the women!

and most especially to Linda Rice-Mandigo

Table of Contents

gooseflesh

The words I want

©Sudie Rakusin 1992

The Words I Want

The words I want do not line up in rows
like obedient school children
They do not raise hands or wait turns
but barge in uninvited
out of breath and foaming at the mouth

The words I want track in mud and earth
and do not make excuses
or clean up after themselves
They do not exit discreetly
but leave holes in walls and stains

The words I want sweat
moan, bleed, spit, get down
and do not give birth immaculately

Fall 1990

Wendy Re-signs

Once she was called Wendy
Child Matriarch of Never-Never Land
Keeper of The Lost Boys
(and other sundry strays)
And she answered the call

She escaped to Never-Never Land
with every other Peter
who offered her smiles:
                    a detachable shadow
                    and a pocket filled with pixie dust
A generous sprinkling and off they flew
to that sacred harbor for perpetual boyhood
where scores of lads had traded "oppression"
under the institution of Motherhood
for a lush fantasy land
where pirates roamed
clockwork crocodiles challenged
and the only rule
was that no one grew up
At last, boys would be boys forever
and ever

The only thing these free boys couldn't conquer
was their own loneliness
And somehow Wendy was responsible
After all, someone had to be
and it couldn't be the boys—
that would ruin the whole thing
and so on and so forth

until . . .

One day Wendy had a dream
When she tried to make sense of her dream
she found no names where she was
for the places she had been
or the things she had seen
She decided she had better check her past
to see if she had left some words behind
But she found that the pixie dust
that fed her fantasies
had robbed her of half her memory

She tried to get off the stuff
But it was no use
and she re-membered the word
for what had happened to her:
            ADDICTION
a word that was never used
in Never-Never Land
How many other words had Wendy forgotten?
There was much that she could not remember
Most of all, Wendy could not remember
how she had lost all those boys
in the first place
and she came to the conclusion
that they all had lost themselves

Then Wendy re-membered a little girl
she had abandoned long ago
because the little girl told "lies"
about all those "good little boys"
that Wendy had lost
Wendy began to feel sick
Then she began to feel smart

When she'd had enough of sick and smart
Wendy began to feel angry
And that was the end of the fairy tale

The little girl introduced herself
as Emma Chavahsdaughter
Once she got off the pixie dust
Chavah realized there were lots of things
that Emma could re-mind her of
And they couldn't fly
but they could climb trees
And they re-membered each other
again and again
until they found some other women
to join them in this ritual called memory
And "Wendy" was the story
they repeated to each other
to re-mind themselves
of the time when they nearly had forgotten
that Eve had any daughters

Winter 1987

Portrait of a Lady

A woman steals
into her apartment,
turns the double bolt
quickly behind her.
She stares back
in frozen panic
at the crack beneath the door—
the gaping mouth
to his world, threatening
to suck her through.
Reaching for a towel,
she stuffs it silent.

A woman tosses
spike-heeled shoes
from swollen feet.
She unclasps
the black cummerbund
from around her waist,
letting blue silk billow:
no longer a prison,
but a sail
sheathing a vital mast.
She breathes roundness
into angular shoulders
fullness into a tabletop belly.

A woman drinks
glass after glass
of cool water, imagining
her cylindrical glass
extends, tube-like
through all seventeen floors
of her building, extends
down into the earth

like the stalk of a plant,
extending its roots
toward the world's network
of oceans and rivers.

A woman bathes her tongue
in vanilla ice cream.
Sucking cold velvet
from the top
of the smooth mound,
she suckles milk
from the full breast
of a new mother;
she drinks in snow
that rests like perspiration
on a mountain top.

A woman cracks nuts
with bare hands.
Bits of broken shell
collect at her feet,
like crumbled china,
as she culls
sweet meat from brittle shell
inside her palm.
She pokes nuts
through waiting lips—
then chews
the rich paste
in thick mouthfuls.

A woman ravages
a bowl of ripe fruits:
becomes ripe,
becomes full.
A woman tears,

Portrait of a Lady

© Sadie Rakusin 1992

with savage teeth,
the sweet flesh from plump figs.
A woman scrapes
white veils
from the pulpy teardrops
of an orange.
She swallows grapes—whole,
gliding down her throat
in tight smooth skins.

A woman
hangs her head in shame
over an empty bowl,
admonishing fingers groping
for the fruits of her indulgence
in her gagging throat—
apologizing, apologizing
apologizing.

Does she grope
for that ancient apple
lodged in her throat?
Does she loosen it
with time and service?
Do her poking fingers
pare it down at all?

Tell me, Adam,
how long is the penance?

Winter 1986

The Poet's Hand

It was the same hand
that never moved
to defend against
her mother's lashes:
the hand that obediently glided
up and down
her cousin's lubricated cock
in calculated rhythm.

It was the same hand
that strummed out scores
of lonely chords
on a twelve string guitar
and scrawled out words
to match the color of rust
on old cast iron:
the smell of the subway
on 110th and Broadway:
the taste of cunt
after a fierce tennis match
in Central Park.

It was the same hand
that braided curls
along her lover's forehead
used a moistened finger
like a tongue
to trace the crannies
of her lover's ear.

The hand that struck
back at no one
and touched another human being

with none but the most gentle intent
was the same hand
that one day found itself
fingering the childproof lid
on a bottle of pills:
popped the cover:
poured the contents
down her own throat
and put herself to sleep
for good.

August 1988.

Chill

I went walking down the street
straight into the lack of you
It left your impression
in gooseflesh on my skin
Now I shudder when the wind blows

Fall 1989

EEG

A little girl sits alone in the dark
She stares at a little green rectangle that blinks
on and off, on and off, over and over
In front of a computer in a well-lit room sits
the testing man She is afraid
that her parents are never coming back

Wires sticking to her head and hands make her feel like the back
of a television set all plugged in to the big dark
armchair Told not to move a muscle or make a noise, she's afraid
even to blink
her eyes So she just sits
quietly and prays for the test to be over

It seems like over
an hour before the testing man comes back
to unplug her and take away the wires He sits
her in his office and questions her about what she saw in the dark
room She tells him about the green blinking
rectangle, but he keeps asking, and she is afraid

she is failing the test She is afraid
of the testing man leaning over
his big desk Squinting her eyes, she makes him blink
on and off, on and off until her parents come back
and the testing man stops staring at her with his dark
stern eyes Everyone worries, although smiles sit

on all their faces like refrigerator magnets Later she sits
in the back seat of her parent's Pontiac, afraid
of their silence She stares out the window at the darkening
sky and knows they will make her do the whole thing over

She doesn't understand how they could send her back
to the testing man, the wires, the dark room and the blinking

rectangle The testing man, the wires and the tiny dark room blink
on and off inside her head as she sits
in the tub and scrubs sticky clay from her head and from the backs
of her hands and cries That night she is afraid
She curses whatever is wrong with her over and over
all night long, awake and afraid, alone in the dark

August 1988

Cleaning Out the Basement Closet

There are yet some things I don't forgive you, Mom
I'm sorting through my childhood belongings:
the stuff to keep, the stuff to give away
I notice things I still will not let go

I'm sorting through my childhood belongings
I find a Planter's peanut can stuffed with colored super-balls
I notice things I still will not let go
Three times I rescue these from the give-away pile

I find a Planter's peanut can stuffed with colored super-balls
What will I do with them now—what did I ever—but collect them
       in a peanut can?
Three times I rescue these from the give-away pile
I remember I had given them each a name

What will I do with them now—what did I ever—but collect them
       in a peanut can?
I collected them because I hated you
I remember I had given them each a name
My collection was a form of retaliation

I collected them because I hated you
You couldn't stand my love for frivolous things
My collection was a form of retaliation
It was all I knew to keep track of who I was

You couldn't stand my love for frivolous things
like the big pink balloon in Central Park
It was all I knew to keep track of who I was
You let go the string while I was on the pony ride

Like the big pink balloon in Central Park,
childhood floated at the end of a string

You let go the string while I was on the pony ride
What did I need it for anyway? you asked my tears

Childhood floated at the end of a string
You never told me you were sorry—it slipped your grasp
What did I need it for anyway? you asked my tears
You didn't see what was in it besides helium

You never told me you were sorry—it slipped your grasp
There are yet some things I don't forgive you, Mom
You didn't see what was in it besides helium:
the stuff to keep, the stuff to give away

Spring 1988

Cold Church Basements

When did it stop working, Annie
What happened
Just before the braided rope
etched death's signature
at your throat
Had the past around you
tightened like a snake
I remember your first meetings
your two black braids, your startled eyes
and stories of the past you couldn't shake
You were Daddy's girl, like me
and threw up all your food in buckets
then ate it back up again
to see if maybe you could get fed
the second time around
But you had come to change all that
go to meetings, chant the slogans
and get well

Was I on my way to work
when you bought that length of rope
driving fast and tapping out the beat
to folk-rock women's latest
while you measured out death
in yards and inches
Did you meet the salesman's eye
hide shame behind a fine-tuned smile
like you did so many times
at Stop and Shop or Friendly's
like we all did
when we ordered our supply
in pounds and quarts
for banquets never planned
and meals already eaten

Why didn't you get better
You came to meetings like the rest
brought love like they said
Every week you came
with your love and your stories
of the one-eyed rabbit
who came to you from nowhere
taught love in parables
and proved to you there was a God
You delighted in her lessons
like the day
you left her cage
filled with freshly cut greens
and she ate away instead
at her own foot

A day here, a day there
you ate three meals
and once you even strung them
into a whole week
But ten years is long to vomit
even with a whole new set of teeth
You loved your little rabbit
came to meetings
"turned your life over"
to the care of something higher
and got tired

Was that it, Annie
Were you just too tired
to sit with me in cold church basements
stirring Lemon Zinger with your pen
or hear me babble any longer
about ex-lovers, miracles and mothers
too tired to believe
the pain won't always last

We told you it would work
But "one day at a time"
it wasn't fast enough for you
So you took your life back
and bought some rope
Annie did you meet the salesman's eye
hide shame behind a smile
Did you carry on in animated tales
as if you planned to dock a boat
or strap a trunk
stuffed wide with bundles
packed up for vacation

Winter 1990

Where it Hurts

Jews are people who love the law
Thou Shalt Not Kill
We crown the Torah in jewels
Thou Shalt Not Steal
We clothe it in finery
Thou Shalt Not Covet Thy Neighbor's Wife
On holy days
we parade it through the shul
for all to kiss
We kiss the law

Thou Shalt Not Bear False Witness
We study texts that debate the law
in endless detail
It is here that I learn
that I am not the "Thou"
in Thou Shalt and Thou Shalt Not
that a man may cast his wife
into the desert if he chooses
that I am impure—not kosher—
when I bleed from my vagina
and must bathe in holy waters
before a man may sleep with me
Not to worry

Thou Shalt Have No Other Gods Before Me
These laws do not speak to me
or to the women that I covet
be they neighbor's wives or not
And yet, when velvet clad
the Torah, clutched in loving arms
strolls through rows of waiting people
I do not turn my back

I do not love this law—or any
But, like I'd dress a child's wound
I add my kiss
I do this because other people spat
on it and us
I do it because other people burned it
and us with it
For more than twenty-four centuries
other people defaced it
tore it, wrapped feces in it
and smeared it with our blood
They made rules, laws and wars
to keep us from our laws and from each other
and my people risked their lives
and still do, to hold it sacred
For over two thousand years
this where it hurt
And so I kiss

Fall 1990
Tishri 5751

Freeze Tag

It's not 'til I'm sitting across from you
in the front seat of your 1971 Ford
and find myself trying to stare a hole
through silence that grips me tighter than a seatbelt
that I realize I know as much about dating
as I do about the mating habits of a codfish

I know about tongues gliding together in mouths
like a pair of dolphins
or tracing circles around firm nipples
like leveling off the top on an ice cream cone
I know that a tongue painting a single stripe
along the lower abdomen
can trap the entire ocean in your womb

But you want to get to know me—
not infuse the space between us
with sexually-induced laughing gas
not escape the labor of newborn intimacy
using sex like anesthesia

but endure the excruciating vulnerability
of just getting to know someone—without sex
of being simultaneously clean, sober and abstinent—and hot
of staying in the moment
when the moment is as tenuous as a soap bubble

It was easy when we were having a carpool and not a DATE
when to touch you was friendly or therapeutic
and to get to know you
was to make background music for a long drive
I don't know how to pose for a get-to-know-you
what to do with my hands and feet

Where only days ago I joked and argued
took pains to explain how and who and why I am
choosing my words like a beachcomber
sifting through pebbles for the choice specimens
I'm now trying to burn a hole through silence with my eyes

The me that assuaged your driver's cramp
one thousand ways in forty hours
warmed away your chills
with the heat of my own ailing body
at the seventeeth rest stop in forty minutes
and tried to heal your colon
through the sore spots in your hands—
that me has now forgotten
how to comb my fingers through your curly locks
or reach my arms around you for a hug

A marionette without strings
I sit wide-eyed and red-lipped
a white-toothed smile painted across my face like a mask
and wait for you
to unfreeze me with a touch

August 1988

Shluf Gezunt

I tiptoe
I tiptoe
because I've kissed
you on the *kepeleh*
and tucked you in for sleep

I tiptoe and I think
about the freckled skin
stretched along your collar bone
the way it falls
in tiny ripples
at your throat
fits your breast
like comfortable clothing
or the skin of an apple
baked to its full sweetness

I talk in whispers
I talk in whispers
because I've kissed
you on the *kepeleh*
and tucked you in for sleep

I talk in whispers and remember
the blessed weight of you:
someone solid to push against
as I rise beneath:
your fingers dipped
between my shivering lips
your body spread like bud-leaves
surrounding a pulsing flower
fat with blooming

I tiptoe and remember
you below:
silver streaks
on flannel pillow
the soft shine
of smooth teeth
framed between lips
parched from rapid breathing
the quaking of your head
the upward reaching
of your chin
as my hand reaches inside you
further than I knew was there
changes shape
and moves to a rhythm
I did not invent

I talk in whispers
and remember side by side:
how firmly we hold on
how lightly our tongues float
like airborne snails
gliding in the airy sea
between two sets
of almost touching lips

I tiptoe
and I feel a flutter:
a songbird trapped
inside my heart
an almost bursting feeling
like too many grapes in your mouth
or a piece of news that won't wait

I talk in whispers
and a pelvic bird
joins my heart bird
I tiptoe
and excited dialogue ensues
like teenagers
on the telephone
They threaten song
But I make them hush

I talk in whispers
an almost bursting feeling
good news that must wait
because I've tucked you
on the *kepeleh*
and kissed you in for sleep

Spring 1989

Shluf Gezunt is Yiddish for Sleep Well
Kepeleh is the Yiddish diminuative for head

I Could Walk

I could say
surprising things too
I could say
out of character things
that show no empathy
I could say,
"take a walk, woman"

or I could translate
what you said
into words that didn't hurt me
on the chance
that you just chose the wrong words

or I could walk away
I could leave you
with your altered state
and your consequences

August 1989

The Laws of Gravity 1

To every action
there is an equal and opposite reaction
even when the reactor knows better
and wishes that she had more self-control

Summer 1990

Skin Code

I woke up
and thought back on my dream
My lover walked in
and saw me musing
She tiptoed over
to where I was sitting
all crooked-like
my eyebrows bent in two directions
compelled by the puzzle of my dream

She got right up onto the bed
put her head in my lap
looked straight up
into my far away eyes
"What are you thinking about?"
she asked as if she had all day to listen
as if she were prepared to follow me
into outer space

I just kept sitting there
quiet like I was
She lifted up her head
level with mind
and began to pet stray curls
off my forehead
She kissed my eyes back into the room
then waited—watching
my gaze spiral home to meet hers

All of a sudden I felt so lucky
I cupped my two palms
around her full cheeks
Against her polished skin

I could feel every ridge
in my own
The way her eyes looked into me
it was as if she were
reading my palms with her cheeks
Braille-style

"I'm so glad you're here,"
I whispered
as I slid the tip of my tongue
across her lip
An indecipherable message
lay on her lips
and in my palms
and just about every place
our skins touched

It's what drew us together;
the need to figure it out I mean
and the need was strong this morning
Understanding nothing
we read with our lips,
our teeth, our tongues,
the tips of our hungry fingers
the code along each other's surfaces

and then I woke up
My lover was standing in the doorway
dressed like she
had somewhere important to go
"Do you realize it's 11:30 a.m. already?"
"Were we supposed to be somewhere?"
I yawned
"Just out in our lives
Isn't that important

enough to wake up for?"
"Is it more real to you out there?"

I looked over
at my lesbian events calendar
pinned on the wall
beside a twenty dollar check—
my first reimbursement for published poetry
Then I spied her unlaced shoes
beside the rocking chair
Emma Goldman's autobiography
pressed open on the pillow
"Isn't this where we live?"

"You know what I mean"
"No," I corrected
"You may find this hard to believe
but some couples actually
spend a good part of their lives
right here in bed."
No Braille now
"I'm sorry," I confessed
"I didn't need to say that.
I just don't like
waking up to accusations"
She said nothing
And then I woke up

I felt like I was bathing
in warm sand It was my lover
wrapping herself around my body
I wasn't sure
which of our gray hair
I was seeing the world through
when I opened my eyes

until I reached
and felt my lover's head

"Let's stay in bed all day today,"
she crooned
I couldn't think
of anything better
As I exhaled
my first deep breath
I felt her arm encircle my belly
There was that code again
And we hadn't yet deciphered it
I smiled because we never would

As she traced the lines
in my soft, tired skin
I knew that I was never dreaming

Fall 1987

Burnt Fingers

I wanted to write about
the way my comb-resistant
brush-resistant hair
turns feather mellow
in your deft fingers

or the patchwork of our skins
mine of fine veined leaf
yours, scaled lizard's coat
snakeskin and gooseflesh
braided in sleep

I wanted them to know
the way your arm around me tightens
when the alarm clock sounds
or what it is we hold
between unflinching, silent eyes
just before you lose me
to the morning

or the way you brush my teeth in bed
when I'm too tired
how I suck the excess toothpaste
from your fingers
or coat your cunt in vinegar
with my tongue's edge

I wanted poems
about all of these
and about how proud
we get with sex
how shy you are in groups
how loud I am at dinner:

quiet dinners
loud, shy sex

but you are gone
This all happens
in my mind's eye only
and my fingers burn already
from touching this

Winter 1990

Gooseflesh   © Sudie Ra Kusin 1992

For Joyce and Barbara

In the warm wake
of the wood stove's residual heat
I sit on burgundy velveteen
and wake up slow

The heat is waning
I pop a eucalyptus drop
and stare into the dark eyes
of the honey-colored dog—
chocolate wrapped in gold paper—
listen to her whine
and wonder how long she'll give me
alone with teacup and book
"It would be nice to have you
here," I tell her,
"your warm weight leaning
thick and heavy into mine"

But then her wet nose
is searching out my face
for something I don't have, I'm sure
Her paws are tangled up in mine
my book has fallen to the floor
my tea is spilling in my lap
and I am searching
for yet another language
to tell her this is not what I want
I wrestle free
and notice cats
They keep more distance—
silent centinels
dykes in uniform,

tall and sleek,
Egyptian statues, only hungrier
I have nothing for their hunger either

This is not my house
I'm sitting in the house of sleeping poets
pets and somebody's ghost—asleep too I think
I'm chilled and getting cramps
I'm wanting a shower
the way the women in the book I'm reading
want each other
The water here wakes up later than I, it seems
and I wonder if anyone will ever wake
and show me how to make it run
hot and clean

And then I don't want them to
I am content here
inside my cramps, inside this house
haunted by poets, pets and ghosts
here in the wake of heat and good conversation
and all I want is to say thank you
Thank you for your poems
and for your chocolate
Thank you for your soft rugs
and unmatched chairs
your pristine kitchen
fresh towels, soft light
and sweet words

I look over at your wood stove
empty-mouthed and hungry
for fresh cut wood
and tell you thank you
Thank you for your fire!

Fall 1990

New Year's Revolution: a Rosh Hashanah Chronology

Rosh Hashanah 1969   5730
Dress Code: pink frill,
black patent shoes w/buckles,
pigtails much too tight
Context: carsick.
Visiting Grandma in "The City;"
much too much food;
much too shy to say anthing.
Homemade cakes (w/pink frill)
displayed on counter top—
reward for those who clean their plates:
ten thousand
tiny bites of gefilte fish
between me and my reward.

Rosh Hashanah 1975   5736
Dress Code: blue corduroy jumper,
itchy tights w/short crotch,
pigtails much too tight
Context: Long Island.
Schools closed.
For once
other kids are glad there are Jews.
At our house,
Grandma has brought her own plate:
too much trouble to kosher ours.
Dad says she's ridiculous.
I don't like any of my food.
Mom says I'm ridiculous.
I'm convinced
gefilte fish and matzo balls
are the same thing in different shapes.

Rosh Hashanah 1981   5742
Dress Code: gray skirt, burgundy sweater,
penny loafers,
hair just short of wild
Context: boarding school.
I'm one of few Jews
who didn't go "home" to be with "family:"
that much more difficult
to negotiate the missed classes:
with each professor a new trial.
But no arguments,
save Professor Schwartz,
who "never did get into that Jewish stuff."
In class
my absence is noticed.
I'm one of few Jews.

Rosh Hashanah 1982   5743
Dress Code: peasant skirt, flannel shirt,
black cotton shoes out of season,
waving hair
revealing no sign of pigtailed past
Context: at "home" with "family."
Rosh Hashanah "conflicted"
with the opening of school,
choice of allegiance left to us.
Why did the resident Rabbi
not see to it
that this "conflict" was avoided?
"Next year will be different,"
he assured me,
"God has handled it for us . . .
The holiday falls on the weekend."
He means the Christian weekend.

In New York City,
I'm choking down gefilte fish,
matzo balls, carrot tsimmes, kugel;
I have forgotten that I detest this food:
anything to pass the time.
In New York City,
I'm choking on scraps of my identity:
anything to get to the dessert

Rosh Hashanah 1987   5748
Dress Code: dress cut,
suitable for weddings and funerals:
colors and pattern
suitable for Wiccan celebration,
black patent shoes (no buckles),
labrys tucked safely under high neck
Context: college campus.
Dinner is potluck.
I have brought my own.
Conversation is a series of questions
directed at me.
"You don't eat any meat?"
". . . no dairy either?"
"How do you get your calcium?"
"and . . . what is that white stuff?"
The subject changes to my name.
"Weren't you called something else
when you were at school here?"
"Do you know the love song, 'Emma'
by Robert Somebody-or-other?"
I grow tired of the inquisition
my labrys growing larger at my throat
"I don't listen to music written by men."
Silence,
followed by another barrage of questions
"No Bob Dylan?" "No Beatles?"
"No rock and roll . . .?!"

The questions blur together.
I'm focused on the necking couple
across the table,
staring pink triangles
into the Magen-Davids
that dangle from gold chains
around their necks.
At synagogue
I take note of the women who sit alone
or with each other.
I am planning next year's Yontiv.

Rosh Hashanah 1989   5750
Dress Code: gray pants, sturdy boots,
cream turtleneck, burgundy sweater,
Magen-David
enameled half yellow, half pink,
hair
exhibiting sharp deviations in length
Context: women.
We sit in a circle
and read from a text we have written ourselves.
Dinner has been a communal effort.
There is mock chicken soup
w/whole wheat matzo balls,
tofu and squash baked into a pie,
a steamed salad
of all the reapings of the Autumn harvest.

We celebrate more than the new year.
We celebrate our plans for a new world:
a world in which Rosh Hashana is a national holiday:
                    in which
people sit in concentric circles at services,
surrounding the Torah, the Rabbi, the cantor,
the interpreter:

in which
we can read along in Hebrew
without the bitter taste of words like
"Kingdom," "Father," "marriage," "punishment:"
        in which
a Magen-David can be purchased at the local jeweler's
one triangle already pink:
        in which
we can close our siddur at the end of the service,
for once, confident
that we shall be inscribed in the book of life!

Fall 1987
Tishri 5748

_____

labrys — pendant replicating battle ax carried by the Amazons
Magen-David — Star of David (Hebrew)
siddur — prayer book (Hebrew)
book of life — During "the days of awe" between Rosh Hashana and
Yom Kippur, it is traditional for Jews to pray to be inscribed in the
"book of life," "the book of health," "the book of prosperity," etc.
When the siddur is closed at the end of the final Yom Kippur service,
it is said that the book is already written for the coming year.

About the Author

At twenty-seven, Emma Morgan is a Jew, a juggler and a lover of words. She says that her poetry and her lesbianism had been hiding in the same closet. Both came out when she was twenty-one, and she has enjoyed reading her work publicly in Northampton (Lesbianville), Massachusetts and its outskirts ever since. Her poems have been published in *Bay Windows, The Wise Woman, Wanting Women: an anthology of erotic lesbian poetry* (Sidewalk Revolution Press) and *Tuesday Night: poetry and fiction by the Valley Lesbian Writer's Group.* She is currently working on her Bachelor's degree at a groovy adult education program in Montpelier, Vermont. Meanwhile, Morgan freelances as a school teacher and dreams of "Liberty and Justice for All."

Clothespin Fever Books

655 4th Ave., Suite 34, San Diego, CA 92101
(619) 234-2656

Are You Girls Traveling Alone? Adventures in Lesbianic Logic by Marilyn Murphy $10.95

Black Slip poems by Terry Wolverton $7.95

Crazy by Carolyn Weathers $8.95

A Dyke's Bike Repair Handbook by Jill Taylor $8.95

Getting Away With Murder by Pele Plante $9.95

Dirty Money by Pele Plante $9.95

In A Different Light: an anthology of Lesbian writers edited by Jenny Wrenn and Carolyn Weathers $9.95

Portraits: Sapphic Zest for Life by Teresita Bosch $8.95

Shitkickers & Other Texas Stories by Carolyn Weathers $7.95

Island of Floating Women by Batya Weinbaum $9.95

Dangerous Ideas by Janet Graham $10.95

Loss of the Ground-Note: women writing about the loss of their mothers edited by Helen Vozenilek $12.95